TELL ME WHY™

The Ocean Is More than a Home for Fish

illustrated by

ROBERT E. WELLS　　**PATRICK CORRIGAN**

Albert Whitman & Company
Chicago, Illinois

For Sarah, Kyle, and Maddox—RW

To my friends and family—PC

Library of Congress Cataloging-in-Publication data is on file with the publisher.
Text copyright © 2023 by Robert E. Wells
Illustrations copyright © 2023 by Albert Whitman & Company
Illustrations by Patrick Corrigan
First published in the United States of America in 2023 by Albert Whitman & Company
ISBN 978-0-8075-7782-0 (hardcover) • ISBN 978-0-8075-7783-7 (ebook)

Printed in China
10 9 8 7 6 5 4 3 2 1 WKT 28 27 26 25 24 23
Design by Shane Tolentino
For more information about Albert Whitman & Company, please visit our website at www.albertwhitman.com.

Earth's plants and animals live in many different places. Most birds build nests in trees. Bats find homes deep inside dark caves. Some fish live in streams and rivers.

Other fish live in the ocean. Our oceans cover about 71 percent of Earth's surface and contain about 97 percent of Earth's water. They are home to more than 16,700 species, or kinds, of fish, including more than 430 species of sharks.

The oceans provide a home for many other kinds of sea creatures too.

Squids and octopuses live in the ocean. So do reptiles such as sea turtles and sea snakes and mammals like whales and dolphins. Birds such as seagulls and most pelicans live close to the oceans and depend on sea life for food.

Phytoplankton are microscopic plants that live near the ocean's surface. They get food and energy directly from the sun. Small, shrimp-like animals called krill feed on the phytoplankton and in turn become food for Earth's biggest creatures, the whales.

close-up of different kinds of phytoplankton

A blue whale, the biggest animal alive, has a heart the size of a small car and a tongue as heavy as an elephant. She feeds by taking in great gulps of seawater full of krill, then expelling the water through her baleen plates, which are made of keratin, like our hair and fingernails, and act as a filter in her mouth. After she expels the water, she swallows the remaining krill.

close-up of krill

The animals and plants that live in the ocean are part of Earth's marine habitat.

Oceanographers, scientists who study oceans, divide the marine habitat into five different oceans: the Pacific, the Atlantic, the Arctic, the Indian, and the Southern.

But the oceans are all connected, and water flows freely among them.

Oceans have different levels, or zones, each suitable for the sea life that lives there. The top 300 feet is the sunlit zone, where most sea creatures live. Below the sunlit zone is the twilight zone, where sunlight barely reaches. Creatures there often have bigger eyes to find their food in the dim light.

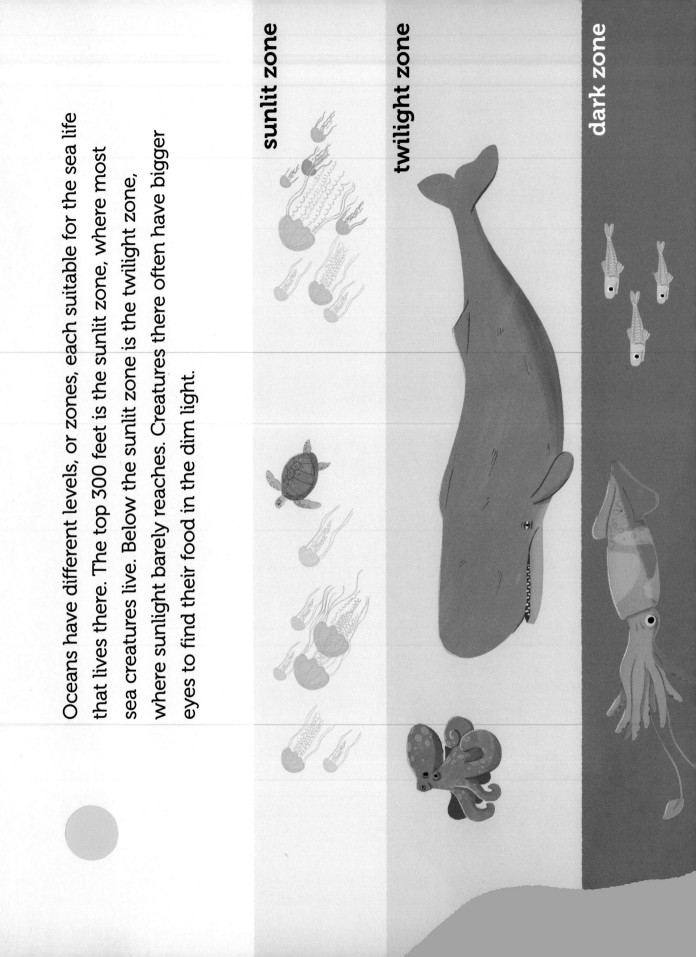

sunlit zone

twilight zone

dark zone

Below the twilight zone is the dark zone, where sunlight does not reach. Many strange but wonderful creatures live there, creating their own light with bioluminescence, a chemical process within their bodies that makes them glow like fireflies.

abyssal plain

Deeper still is the abyssal plain, where life is scarce in the near-freezing darkness. There are also trenches in the abyssal plain where the ocean is about 7 miles deep.

Coral reefs are mainly located in the sunlit zones of tropical oceans. They are important to people in many ways. They support about one-quarter of all sea life, which in turn provides food for millions of people.

Some corals also produce chemicals that are valuable in the treatment of many human illnesses, such as heart disease and cancer. The rigid structure of the reef also helps protect coastlines from erosion.

Can you imagine how much water is in Earth's oceans? Imagine a giant fishbowl 40 miles wide, full of ocean water. That's a lot of water. But its just a start.

It would take almost eight thousand of those giant fishbowls to hold all of Earth's ocean water—and if those fishbowls were stacked one on top of the other, they would reach to the moon!

Although 97 percent of Earth's water is ocean salt water,
3 percent of Earth's water is fresh water that is available for life
on land, because of Earth's water cycle.

Earth's water cycle begins with the sun. Heat changes both
fresh water and ocean water into its gas form, called water vapor,
through a process called evaporation.

The water vapor rises, because it is lighter than the surrounding air, and forms clouds. When ocean water evaporates, the salt stays in the ocean. It is heavier than air, so it does not rise.

Wind, which is caused when cold air moves into areas where warmer air has risen, blows some clouds over land. When the air temperature cools, the clouds' water droplets grow larger and heavier. When they become too heavy to remain in the clouds, they fall as rain.

The rain that falls on land supplies fresh water for all living things on land. Streams and rivers return some of the rainfall back into the ocean, where it evaporates again, completing Earth's water cycle.

The ocean is always moving, and there are many currents that flow along its surface. Water can be either warm or cold, and when it flows along land, some of its warmth or coolness radiates to the land.

One of the ocean's surface currents is the Gulf Stream in the Atlantic Ocean. It helps circulate warm water from the equator and cold water from the Arctic to both sides of the ocean, helping to keep the climate of the land on both sides more comfortable for the people and animals who live there.

Ocean currents also help ships transport their cargo to the world's seaports. Cargo ships sail across the oceans every day, carrying containers filled with products from nearly every nation. About 90 percent of all the world's trade travels by ocean. When ships travel with the help of ocean currents, they save fuel—and weeks of travel time.

The ocean does many important things for people. It provides food and medicine, makes our land more comfortable, and is a central part of Earth's water cycle. Because it is so valuable, we must take care of it.

For most of Earth's history, our atmosphere has contained a just-right amount of carbon dioxide, a colorless gas that absorbs and stores heat. But the number of cars, trucks, airplanes, and factories has greatly increased in recent years, putting more carbon dioxide into the air and upsetting the just-right balance.

Ocean water absorbs and stores much of the extra carbon dioxide from the air, causing the ocean to become warmer. The carbon dioxide also creates acid in the ocean water. The higher temperatures, as well as the acid, harm coral reefs and the sea creatures that depend on them by disrupting their normal environment.

The extra heat in the oceans also gives more energy to ocean storms that can move onto land, causing destruction in cities, towns, and villages.

In addition to carbon dioxide, discarded plastic bottles and bags also cause damage to sea life. Animals mistake plastic for food, so the plastic gets into their stomachs and stays there, and seabirds become entangled by plastic bags. Countries all over the world are working together to reduce the damage caused by plastic waste and other kinds of ocean pollution.

One important way everyone can help is to recycle or reuse the plastic bottles and bags we use in our homes so they do not end up in the ocean.

If we all do a small part to help take care of our ocean, it will help the ocean continue to be a good home for sea creatures—and that will make Earth a better and healthier home for people and animals on land.

Glossary

acid: A substance that can be harmful to life.

carbon dioxide: A heavy, colorless gas that absorbs and stores heat.

climate: The typical weather in a certain place.

energy: The power that causes movement or change.

erosion: The process of wearing away due to the motion of water, wind, or glacial ice.

evaporation: The process of turning a liquid into vapor, or gas.

mammal: A warm-blooded animal, usually covered with fur or hair, whose young are fed on their mother's milk.

marine: Relating to the ocean.

microscopic: Something so small it can be seen only with a microscope.

reptile: A cold-blooded animal, such as a turtle, lizard, or snake, that is often covered with scales or hard plates.

tropical: Relating to the warm areas of the world surrounding the equator.

Selected Sources

Brown, Laaren. *Ocean Animals*. New York: Liberty Street, 2015.

French, Jess. *Earth's Incredible Oceans*. New York: DK Publishing, 2021.

Gray, Susan H. *Oceanography: The Study of Oceans*. New York: Children's Press, 2012.

Henzel, Cynthia Kennedy. *Great Barrier Reef*. Edina, MN: ABDO, 2011.

MacQuitty, Miranda. *Eyewitness Ocean*. New York: DK Publishing, 2014.

Parker, Steve. *Ocean and Sea*. New York: Scholastic, 2012.

Twist, Clint. *The Oceanology Handbook: A Course for Underwater Explorers*. Somerville, MA: Templar, 2010.